YOU CAN

grow your own food

Annabelle Padwick

CONTENTS

YOU CAN GROW YOUR OWN FOOD

Growing your own food is really fun!
This book will give you loads of inspiration so that
YOU CAN grow all your favourite fruit and vegetables.

Find some soil, pick up a packet of seeds, a watering
can and a trowel, and prepare to grow your own food!
This book is full of activities you can do in your own
garden, in a shared allotment, on a balcony, or on your
windowsill – you don't need your own garden to grow
your own food!

There are activities for everyone – whether you want
to create a pizza garden, grow a bean den or just feel
proud picking your own homegrown, tasty food.

There are lots of spaces in the book for you to record
your activities, create lists, add photos and design your
own garden. So what are you waiting for? Read on,
and then go and grow your own food!

So why is growing your own food so good?

⭐ You can choose which fruit and vegetables you eat.

⭐ You can grow varieties you may not see in the supermarket.

⭐ You can pick produce straight from the plant, reduce plastic waste and cut down the pollution from transporting food across the planet.

⭐ You can get muddy and have fun!

Why do you want to grow your own food?

Now turn the page and start growing your own food!

EQUIPMENT

Before you can start growing your own food, there are a few things that you need so your plants grow happily and so that you are safe.

 GLOVES

Some plants have thorns or rough stems that may hurt your skin, so it's always best to wear gloves. If you are handling shop-bought compost, pop them on as well. This reduces the chance of you getting an infection in any small cuts or grazes.

COMPOST

If you are growing your own food in containers and don't have a compost bin at home, then you will need to fill them with multi-purpose compost. You can buy big bags from your local garden centre.

You can learn how to make your own compost on page 86.

TROWEL AND FORK

You can use these super handy tools to help you dig holes for planting and to fill pots with compost.

Other tools you may need are a spade, rake, and hoe.

WATERING CAN

Just like you, all plants need water to survive and grow. Choose a watering can with a rose head attachment like this one, so your compost, seeds and small plants don't get washed away or damaged.

SEEDS OR PLANTS

Have a read through this book, decide what you would like to grow and make a list on page 24. You will find many seeds and plug plants in your local garden centre, so save up some money and head there.

Plug plants are baby plants that have been started off for you. You don't get the excitement of seeing your seeds pop up through the soil, but they may be easier for you to grow.

SPACE

You don't need lots of space to start growing your own food.

You can have a patch at the back of your garden, a raised bed or a collection of containers – there are different options, as you can see.

You can grow your plants in nearly anything – from buckets and grow bags, to wellington boots and old bath tubs.

Have a look around and see what you can find!

Make sure whatever container you choose is deep enough for the roots to get established and that it has drainage holes. Any excess water needs to escape so your plants don't become waterlogged. If you need help to make some holes in the bottom of a container, just ask an adult to help you with a drill or scissors.

If you don't have space for containers, or access to a garden, you could ask friends and family about going with you to a community garden or allotment. Many towns have them, and for free, or a small fee, you can grow your own produce and still try out the activities in this book. You may make some new friends as well.

Add a photo or draw a picture here of the space where you will grow your own food.

SOIL TYPES

Your soil is very important if you want to grow lots of yummy fruits and vegetables. It needs to be full of nutrients to feed your plants and help them grow.

Great soil, full of goodness and life, comes from four sources.

ORGANIC MATTER, such as manure, vegetable peelings, grass cuttings, old paper and fruit trimmings.

MINERAL SOLIDS, such as sand, silt and clay, help provide an anchor for the plants and their roots.

Use this box to record any creepy crawly findings.

Fungi are very important for many plants, especially those grown in woodlands and gardens. Plants borrow the roots of the fungi nearby to hold extra water and create a stronger base in the ground. As a thank you, the plant naturally gives nutrients back to the fungi.

PLANT STRUCTURE

Fruit and vegetable plants can look very different, but most have the same physical features.

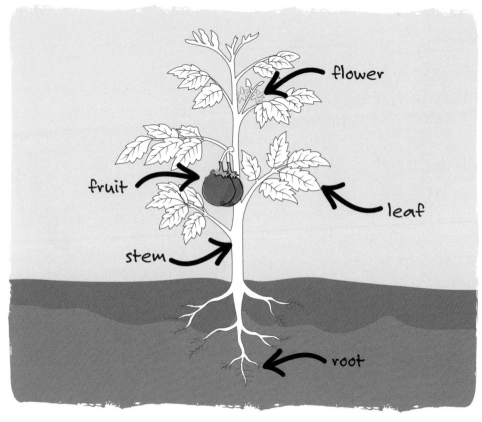

When you sow a seed in the soil, it will germinate into a tiny plant called a seedling. This is the start of the stem, which will shoot up into the air reaching for sunlight. Leaves will then form, and these turn sunlight into the energy needed for the plant to survive.

Under the ground, roots will form, spreading out downwards in the search for food and water. The roots will suck up all the nutrients, helping the plant to grow and stay healthy.

You will learn more about fruits and vegetables as you go through this book. Discover how some grow above the ground, like tomatoes, courgettes and sweetcorn. Others, like carrots, potatoes and beetroot, grow under the ground, forming as part of the root.

tomatoes

carrots

As you start watching your plants grow, see if you can identify the different parts.

TIP!

Always handle seedlings gently by the leaves to keep them happy and healthy. If you accidentally snap the leaves, the plant can still continue to grow.

GETTING STARTED

You now know all the fun things about soil and what you need to begin growing your own food.

Here are a couple more tips that will help get you started.

FILLING PLANT POTS

Some of the activities in this book will need a plant pot filled with multi-purpose compost.

What to do

1 Scoop or spoon compost into your pot, leaving a 1–2 cm gap at the top. You don't want to fill the pot up to the top, otherwise the water has nowhere to sit and sink through to your plant.

2 Break up any lumps in the compost using your hands. Seeds need fine soil so that they can germinate and reach the surface easily.

3 Gently press the compost down to make sure the surface is level.

SOWING SEEDS

You can sow seeds into filled plant pots or directly into your garden. The seed packets and activities in this book will tell you what to do and how, but here are some basic tips.

⭐ Always read the instructions on the seed packet!

⭐ Water the compost or soil well before sowing seeds.

Small seeds like lettuce and carrots need to be sown 1–2 cm under the surface of the compost, as they grow delicate stems that can only push through a thin layer.

Big seeds like pumpkins and beans need to be buried deep under the surface, 3–4 cm. They need more compost to support their strong stems.

POTTING ON

If you can see roots coming out of the bottom of your small plant pot then it's time to move your plant into a bigger pot. This process is called 'potting on'.

This task will allow your plants to spread their roots and take on more water and food from the compost.

What to do

1 Fill your new large pot with compost, then make a hole in the middle the same size as your old pot.

2 Hold the plant in one hand and turn it over in the pot so that it is resting on your other hand.

3 Carefully pull away the pot – if it gets stuck, gently squeeze the pot and give it a wiggle!

4 Keep your fingers either side of the stem or hold the leaves – you do not want to hold the stem in case it breaks.

5 Place the plant into its new big pot. Gently press it down so it sits happy and level in the soil.

6 Water your new potted plant.

You can also follow these tips if you have 2 healthy plants in one small pot. Carefully tease the roots apart using your fingers and give each plant its own pot so they can both grow big and strong.

WATERING

All plants need water to live and grow!
Here are some top tips.

⭐ Always use a watering can to pour water over the surface of the compost.

⭐ Plants prefer rainwater to tap water, so leave a few buckets outside. When it rains, they will fill up and you can use them to fill your watering can.

⭐ Always water around the plant and not on to leaves or flowers! Don't panic if a few droplets touch the plant, but always try to get as much on the soil as you can.

⭐ Water plants in the morning or evening. In the afternoon it is generally warmer, so water may dry out before it soaks into the compost.

⭐ Poke your finger into the compost. If it feels wet then you don't need to water. If it feels dry, then add more water.

Drooping leaves are a sign that your plant needs water!

21

PLANT FEED

Most plants love being fed every 2 weeks so that they get lots of nutrients to form plenty of leaves, flowers and fruits.

Plants need nitrogen – to help with leaf growth – and potassium, which helps the plants flower and grow fruits like tomatoes.

You can buy nitrogen and potassium plant feed from your local garden centre. Making your own is much more fun and better for the environment. They can be a bit smelly, though!

TIP!

Nettles make a strong nitrogen feed, but be careful that they don't sting you when you're picking the leaves!

COMFREY FEED

Comfrey is rich in potassium, so perfect for making plant feed.

What to do

1 Wearing gloves, collect lots of comfrey leaves.

2 Rip them up and place them in a pot with a drainage hole. Put the pot inside a bucket with a tight lid.

3 You can use a rock to hold down the leaves.

4 Add water until the leaves are completely covered, then pop the lid on.

5 After 6 weeks, hold your nose and open the lid!

6 Remove the pot so all the liquid drains into the bucket.

7 Put one cup of the smelly liquid into a watering can, then add 10 cups of water.

8 Water your plants!

comfrey

Right... let the fun begin – it's time to start growing your own food!

START PLANNING

Now it's time to decide which of your favourite fruits and vegetables you would like to grow at home. All plants need different conditions, so have a look through the book and see if you can find them listed. If not, ask an adult to check for you. Oranges, lemons, mangoes, bananas and other tropical fruits need special, hot conditions, so may not be possible to grow at home.

What would you like to grow?

EQUIPMENT CHECKLIST

Use this page to make sure you have everything you need. Start by ticking the items you have at home.

As you do the activities, you may need other tools and equipment, so use this space to also write a shopping list.

Equipment	Got it?
Gloves	
Trowel	
Fork	
Watering can	
Pots – if growing in containers	
Compost – if growing in containers	
Seeds	

ACTIVITIES

GROW A PIZZA GARDEN

Do you love pizza? Growing fresh, tasty toppings for your own pizza can be super easy. You can grow them in containers, or how about designing your own circular bed in the garden with every pizza wedge shape of soil having a different topping?

Buy small plants or sow your favourite toppings from seed and watch them grow into big healthy plants – it's great fun!

Tasty toppings you could try:

- ✹ **TOMATOES** – need a bright, sunny spot, regular watering and feeding.

- ✹ **BASIL** – likes lots of sun and regular watering.

- ✹ **ROCKET** – needs sunshine for 4–5 hours a day and regular watering.

- ✹ **COURGETTES** – need full sunshine, regular watering and feeding.

- ✹ **PEPPERS** – love lots of sunshine, regular watering and feeding.

You could also try onions, sweetcorn, oregano, chillies and spinach.

Now it's time to think about your pizza garden. Consider how the different colours, scents and tastes will look together, like bright red tomatoes next to bold green basil. You can also grow purple basil!

DID YOU KNOW?

You can make your own plant feed. Have a look at page 22 for more information.

Design and draw your own pizza garden here.

29

MAKE SEED TAPES

Sowing seeds directly in the ground can sometimes be a little tricky, especially if you only want to sow a few seeds.

One way to make sure you don't sow too many seeds in the same place is to make seed tapes.

What to do

1 Cut strips of paper about 2 cm wide.

2 Fold the strips in half lengthways:

```
.........................................................
```

3 On the seed packet of your chosen seeds it will tell you how far apart the seeds need to be sown. Using a ruler and pencil, mark along one half of the strip, spacing the marks at the distance required.

4 Using a brush, place a spot of the flour and water glue on each pencil mark.

5 Pick one seed at a time off the plate using a damp brush and place it onto the glue.

6 Fold over the other half of the paper strip to encase the seeds. Leave it to dry on a flat surface, like a table or windowsill.

7 Use an envelope to store the folded tape. Don't forget to write your name and the seed type on it.

8 When it's sowing time, place your seed tapes in the soil, cover them with more soil, then water the area. Make a plant label using the instructions on page 40 and water your seeds regularly.

You'll need:

* strips of cheap paper about 2 cm wide
* a plate with seeds
* a ruler
* a pencil
* a brush
* flour and water glue
* envelopes

GROW CRESS HEADS

You can grow these little faces with edible hair indoors on a windowsill. You just need a few things!

What to do

1 Eat a boiled egg with the top cut off, or ask someone else to.

2 Wash the egg shell and dry with tissue.

3 Decorate the outside of your shell with a funny face!

4 Place the cotton wool in the egg shell and give it a spray of water.

5 Sprinkle on your cress seeds!

6 You can now place your egg shell in an egg cup on a sunny windowsill so the seeds can germinate.

You'll need:
* cotton wool
* cress seeds
* an egg shell
* a pen
* tissue

Practise drawing your funny face here before drawing it on the egg shell.

TIP!

Don't have an egg cup? Make one with a 3 cm wide strip of card! Just wrap it into a cylinder and use a small piece of sellotape to stick the ends together.

WELLY PLANTERS

Don't let anyone throw away your old wellies! Boots are great as containers in the garden or on a balcony. They look fun and can grow really tasty food! So how do you make them? Easy!

What to do

1 Wash the outside of your wellies with warm, soapy water, then dry them with a towel. You want your wellies to look fab!

2 Ask an adult to drill four holes in the bottom of the boots. This is so water can drain out of the bottom when you water your plants.

3 You can place pebbles in the bottom of your wellies to make sure they don't blow over. This will also create better drainage.

4 Fill the boots with multi-purpose compost until you reach roughly 6 cm from the top.

5 Now it's time to sow your favourite seeds or pop in some plants.

6 Add a bit more compost and give your wellies some water.

7 All finished – now it's time to pop them in the sunshine!

Check the seed packet or plant label to find out if your chosen plants like full sun, shade or a bit of both! Position your wellies in the correct spot to get the best plants.

Don't forget to water them regularly!

Containers can dry out quickly on sunny, warm days, so be sure to water them every other day during the summer.

Create your own list of everything you will need:

- wellies

GROW EDIBLE FLOWERS

Did you know that you can eat certain types of flowers? Let's have a look at a few of them.

NASTURTIUM

Super colourful and tasty!

Sow seeds from March to May, 20 mm deep in the soil where you would like them to grow. Keep rows 30 cm apart and water the seedlings regularly as they grow into strong, bright plants.

Lots of different colours flower from summer to autumn: cream, oranges, yellows and reds. Pick their peppery petals and add them to your homegrown salads.

ROSE

You can eat the petals of all roses. Why not use them to decorate a cake, add to drinks, or pop them in an ice tray for pretty ice cubes?

DAISY

You will see daisies in many gardens and parks, but did you know that the petals can be eaten and added as decoration to salads and cakes?

COURGETTE

The flowers that grow at the end of courgettes can be eaten in many ways.

- Dip them in batter and fry in a pan.

- Add them to hot pasta sauces.

- Eat cold, stuffed with cooked rice, beans, nuts or cheese.

What are your favourite edible flowers?

You can also eat lavender, borage, chamomile, sunflowers and elderflowers!

MAKE A BEAN DEN

Want to plan exciting adventures and write imaginative stories whilst nibbling on veggies that you have grown? Create your own den covered in climbing beans! You may need the help of an adult to build the frame, but the planting and den is all yours.

What to do

1 Find a big, clear space in the garden.

2 Space the canes in a circle, each at least 30 cm apart. You want the circle in the middle to be big enough for you and perhaps a friend to sit in.

3 Ask an adult to push the bottom of the canes into the soil at an angle and tie them together at the top with the string.

4 You can now dig a hole at the base of each cane and sow 3 bean seeds. Cover them over with soil and give them lots of water.

5 Water them every couple of days and feed them weekly when flowers appear. You can read about feeding plants and making your own feed on page 22.

You'll need:

⭐ 10–20 bamboo or willow canes – you can buy these at garden centres
⭐ string or twine
⭐ runner bean seeds
⭐ a tape measure (not essential)

What will you do in your den? Write stories, play games or eat beans? Plan your adventures here.

TIP!

For a happy den and plants, pick your beans gently – try not to leave the top of the bean on the plant. The more beans you pick, the more will grow!

PEBBLE PLANT LABELS

You can make your own personalised plant labels so that you never forget what you have planted.

What to do

1 Start by choosing which plants you need labels for. Make a list.

2 Cover a table or the floor with sheets of newspaper to protect them from the paint.

3 Get painting!

4 Leave your pebbles to dry before placing them outside next to your rows of seeds and growing fruits and vegetables.

You'll need:

* pebbles
* garden paints
* paintbrushes
* a cup of water (to wash your brushes!)
* newspaper
* a selection of freshly planted fruit and vegetable plants

Use this space to practise the design that you'll paint on your pebbles.

TIP!

You could pick paint colours that match the fruits and vegetables your pebbles are for.

GROW YOUR OWN CHIPS

Do you like chips? How about dipped in tomato ketchup? Well, did you know that you can grow and make your own? Even the ketchup if you wanted!

DID YOU KNOW?

Chips are made from potatoes, just like mash!

Start growing them in April and you will have your own potatoes to turn into chips by the summer holidays. Have a look at page 64 for how to grow your own potatoes.

Now to turn your potatoes into chips!

1 Preheat the oven to 220°C / 200°C Fan / Gas 7.

2 Cut the potatoes into long 1.5 cm-wide strips, so they look like chips. You can ask a grown-up to help you.

3 Place the cut potatoes into a mixing bowl and add 1 tablespoon of oil.

4 Give them a good stir with a spoon or get your hands in if you don't mind getting messy.

5 Place on a baking tray and bake in the oven for 20–25 minutes.

6 Remove from the oven with the help of an adult when golden brown.

Choose a variety of potatoes:

* Maris Piper
* Russet
* Cara
* King Edward

TIP!

Using an old toothbrush or nail brush will help remove any soil on the potato.

You can add homegrown herbs to your mix if you want to give your chips a different flavour.

If you have some smaller potatoes, just turn them into wedges!

GROW A HERB GARDEN

Herbs are super easy to grow and they don't need that much attention. You can grow herbs in pots or in the ground, so your herb garden can be as big or small as you like. Many herbs will grow inside or outside too!

There are so many herbs to choose from, all with different tastes and smells. Some even have healing properties if you are feeling poorly.

You can grow many herbs from seed, which will take more time and patience, but will be very exciting!

- coriander
- basil
- bay plant
- chive
- coriander
- dill
- fennel
- golden oregano
- lavender
- mint
- parsley
- rosemary
- sage
- tarragon
- thyme
- wild garlic

All herbs love sunshine and regular feeding but can need different soil conditions. Some herbs like wet soil with regular watering and others only need watering when the soil dries out completely.

WET HERBS: mint, thyme, watercress, sorrel, lemon balm, chervil
DRY HERBS: rosemary, oregano, lavender, basil, sage, tarragon

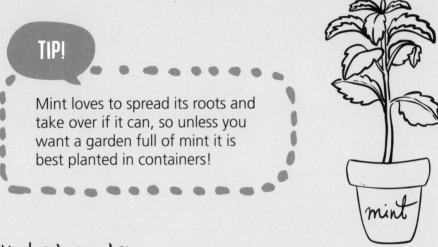

TIP!

Mint loves to spread its roots and take over if it can, so unless you want a garden full of mint it is best planted in containers!

mint

My herb garden

Herb	Date planted	Tasty? Score 1-10!

Turn over to see how you can eat your homegrown herbs!

USING YOUR HERBS

Basil is really yummy with tomatoes! You can pop it on pizza when it comes out of the oven, have it on a fresh tomato salad, or you can add it to pasta sauce.

Thyme is great with roast potatoes – just pop some in the baking tray.

Mint is delicious in cold drinks! You can also add it to watermelon and feta cheese for a yummy salad. Make your own mint sauce for a roast dinner too!

Parsley is fantastic mixed with potato and salmon to make fishcakes.

Jot down how you'll use your herbs here.

GROW & MAKE A WINTER STEW

Winter stews are great to eat after a long day playing outdoors in the cold. They are delicious and warm you up quickly!

Winter stews are super easy, tasty meals that will help keep away coughs and colds!

Tasty ingredients you could include:

- **POTATO** – grow in grow bags, large containers or outside directly in the soil. Read how to grow these on page 64.

- **TOMATO** – grow in tomato grow bags, containers or outside directly in the ground. Read how to grow these on page 67.

- **CARROT** – grow in 30 cm containers or outside directly in the ground. Read how to grow these on page 59.

- **ONION** – grow in large 50 cm containers or directly outside in the soil.

- **PUMPKIN** – grow outside directly in the ground. Read how to grow these on page 76.

You can also add beans, kale, parsnips, lentils, herbs or meat – anything you like really!

What to do

1 Ask a grown-up to help chop the vegetables and warm up the oil in a large pan. Then add the onions.

2 After 5–6 minutes, you can add the leeks, carrots, swede and parsnips.

3 Give them all a stir!

4 Add the barley, apple juice, vegetable stock, thyme and parsley.

5 Stir again!

6 Put a lid on the pan and allow the vegetables to cook for 45 minutes. Stir every 15 minutes to help stop them sticking.

7 Spoon your homemade stew into your favourite bowls!

You'll need:

* 1 tablespoon olive oil
* 350 g onions – chopped
* half a swede – chopped into chunks
* 350 g carrots – chopped
* 2 parsnips – chopped
* 2 leeks – sliced
* 175 g pearl barley
* 3 tablespoons apple juice
* 1 l vegetable stock
* 2–3 sprigs thyme
* handful of parsley – chopped

If you don't like any of the vegetables listed, just swap them with your favourites that you are growing! Just remember to give all the vegetables a good wash in a bowl of water before you start chopping and making your stew. You don't want any soil or bugs in your dinner!

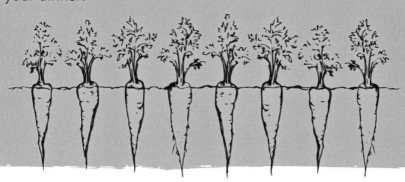

GROW LEAFY CATERPILLARS

Make your own mini containers that will fit perfectly on your windowsill. You can decorate them to look like caterpillars – or whatever design you would like.

What to do

1 Lay down sheets of newspaper onto a table so you protect the surface.

2 Decorate your egg boxes to look like caterpillars: how about eyes and feet?

3 Place a small piece of cotton wool in the bottom of each egg hole, then add a teaspoon of compost.

4 Sow 2–3 seeds into each egg hole.

5 Cover the seeds with more compost.

6 Water and place on a windowsill or in a greenhouse.

7 When the compost feels dry, add a few more sprinkles of water.

8 Cut some of your salad leaves when ready and enjoy snacking!

You'll need:

* compost
* cotton wool
* egg boxes – cut into strips
* glue
* lettuce, rocket or cress seeds
* newspaper
* pens
* wiggly eye stickers

As your plants grow and
need more nutrients,
you can pot them on
into a larger container.
They may last longer in a
bigger pot too!

Take a photo of your creation and stick it here.

PEAS AND BEANS

Runner beans, French beans, broad beans, sugar snap peas, petit pois peas and many more types of beans are all part of a family called 'legumes'.

You can grow really tall varieties, like French bean 'Cobra' or pea 'Alderman', shooting up way above your head. Dwarf Purple French bean 'Amethyst' and 'Delikett' peas are great short varieties, perfect for containers.

HOW TO GROW BEANS AND PEAS

1 In April–May, fill 7–8 cm pots with multi-purpose compost.

2 Sow 1–2 seeds per pot, about 5 cm deep.

3 Give them plenty of water using a watering can.

4 Place on a sunny windowsill indoors and in approximately 15 days, you should see tiny plants popping up through the soil.

5 Keep watering your seedlings regularly and plant outside in June when they have strong stems and leaves.

TIP!

Don't have space inside? Wait until late May or early June – then you can sow your bean and pea seeds directly outside.

You can keep track of the types of beans and peas you have grown by using a table like the one below.

Variety	Sown date	Harvest date	Tasty? Score 1–10!

BUILD A SUPPORT

If you have chosen climbing or tall varieties of peas or beans, they will need a support for their tendrils (thin stems) to cling on to and climb.

What to do

1 Ask a grown-up to push the canes into the ground at a slight angle and 30 cm apart.

2 Tie them together at the top using the string or twine.

3 Add netting to the frame for peas so they have more area for their tiny tendrils to take hold.

You'll need:

* bamboo canes
* string or twine
* netting for peas

Don't forget to keep watering your plants and start feeding them fortnightly as flowers appear.

You can easily make an A-shaped frame or wigwam with the help of an adult.

If you have chosen a dwarf or container variety, you can still make a mini wigwam using collected sticks and twigs.

BRASSICAS

Lots of leafy vegetables belong to a family called 'brassicas'.
Can you name all of these?

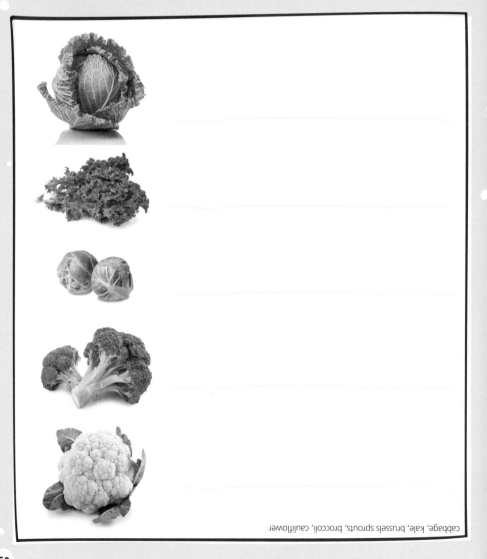

cabbage, kale, brussels sprouts, broccoli, cauliflower

All members of the Brassica family need to be grown directly in the ground. You can start them off in pots or trays though until they are big and strong enough for planting. You don't want them getting eaten by slugs and birds!

How to grow cabbages, broccoli, brussels sprouts, cauliflower and kale

1 In February–April, fill 7–8 cm pots or seed trays with multi-purpose compost.

2 Sow 1–2 seeds per pot, about 1.5 cm deep.

3 Give them plenty of water using a watering can.

4 Place on a sunny windowsill indoors or in a greenhouse. In approximately 15 days, you should see tiny plants popping up through the soil.

Keep watering your seedlings regularly and plant outside in June–July, when they have strong stems and leaves.

TIP!

Space your seedlings according to the individual seed packets when planting in the ground. It can vary from 30 cm for cabbages to 75 cm for brussels sprouts.

WHEN TO HARVEST

The seed packet will tell you when to harvest your leafy veggies. This varies between September and December.

CABBAGE WHITE BUTTERFLIES

Brassicas are loved by cabbage white butterflies, but these beautiful creatures are not good for your plants. You can pick their eggs and the hungry caterpillars off plants to avoid any disappearing leaves and giant holes. The best way to protect your cabbages and other leafy vegetables is netting.

You can buy netting from your local garden centre. Pick the one which has lots of tiny gaps so butterflies and pigeons can't get in.

You should place the netting over your plants straight after planting them in the ground.

Record your progress using the table below.

Variety	Sown date	Harvest date	Tasty? Score 1-10!

CARROTS

Do you like these orange, crunchy delights? Did you know that there are also purple varieties like 'Purple Sun'?!

Carrots are a type of root vegetable. We eat the swollen root of root vegetables, that's how they get their group name.

Carrots like light soil with not many stones. Stones or big lumps will cause your carrots to fork and become a funny shape.

If you notice lots of lumps and don't want carrots that look like monsters, you can use a rake or fork to break them up!

Sow carrots directly in the ground or in 30 cm containers outside from March to July. Place your seeds 1 cm deep in the soil and in rows 20–30 cm apart. Water them every 2 days.

If you grow carrots in containers then don't worry about rows. Just sprinkle the seeds thinly across the surface of the compost, then cover with another 1 cm.

When are they ready for digging up? Depending on when you sow your carrots, you can harvest them from the summer time. Just pull a single carrot first to check its size. They will last in the ground until late autumn.

RADISHES

Radishes are super speedy to grow. Remove their leafy tops and they look like balloons!

Radishes are crunchy and taste a little spicy – a bit like pepper.

What to do

1 Grow radishes outside in containers at least 30 cm deep.

2 Fill up your containers with multi-purpose compost; leave a 10 cm gap at the top.

3 Sprinkle your radish seeds over the surface, and then cover them with 1 cm of compost.

4 Give them plenty of water and keep them watered every 2 days.

5 Pull your radishes up gently when they are just a bit bigger than a marble.

BEETROOT

They stain your fingers, tongue and clothes with their bright purple colour, but beetroot are super tasty! You can grow varieties like 'Boltardy' and 'Boston' which have that bright pop of colour, or 'Burpees Golden' which isn't purple or red – it's a golden yellow colour!

Sow beetroot directly outside in the ground where you want them to grow. You can sow seeds in rows 30 cm apart from March to July, placing them 3 cm deep in the soil.

beetroot seeds

Germination can take up to 24 days, so you may need to be patient. Keep watering the rows when the soil is dry and you will soon have beetroot leaves popping up through the surface.

DID YOU KNOW?

You can bake beetroot or roast it in a pan. It's not just for salads and is really tasty eaten warm. You can also make beetroot crisps!

When are they ready for digging up? When they are the size of a golf ball!

PARSNIPS, SWEDE AND TURNIPS

Parsnips are delicious roasted, and swedes and turnips are great for stews!

Parsnips take a long time to grow, so start sowing these in March–April. Swede and turnips can be sown from March until June.

Just like carrots, all other root vegetables like light soil with no big lumps.

Sow their seeds thinly 1 cm deep in soil, with 30 cm between your rows.

TIP!

Keep the soil between your vegetables weed free by picking out any tiny weeds as they pop up. Root vegetables love lots of water, so try not to let the soil dry out.

When are they ready for digging up? Pull up parsnips after the first frost in autumn. Swede and turnips are ready when they are between golf and tennis ball size.

Use the table below to record your progress growing root vegetables.

Variety	Sown date	Harvest date	Tasty? Score 1-10!

POTATOES

Do you love treasure hunts? If so, you will love growing potatoes as you have to go hunting in the soil to find them!

Potatoes are very easy to grow, either in containers or in the ground.

'Chit' your seed potatoes to give them a head start. All you have to do is place your seed potatoes (you can buy seed potatoes from a garden centre) in a tray or old egg box with the eyes facing upwards. Leave them on a windowsill for 4–6 weeks and shoots will start to appear.

eyes

Growing in containers

1 Fill ⅓ of your potato grow bag with compost.

2 You can plant 3–4 seed potatoes per bag.

3 Place them on top of the soil with the eyes pointing upwards.

4 Cover the potatoes with compost.

5 As new growth emerges through the top of the compost, add more compost and keep covering the growth until you are near the top of the bag. Gradually adding compost over the new growth (rather than filling the bag up straight away) helps grow more potatoes!

6 Potatoes love lots of watering and also a fortnightly feed.

7 You can go hunting for your potatoes as soon as the flowers die back and the leaves turn brown.

You'll need:

* potato grow bags
* seed potatoes
* compost

GROWING IN THE GROUND

Growing potatoes in the ground is simple too. Just dig a hole at least 15 cm deep and place in 1 potato with the eyes facing upwards. Do the same for the rest of your potatoes, then cover them all over with soil.

As the new growth emerges, cover them up with more soil so you create a mound. Once you have a mound 8–10 cm high, you can stop and just keep watering your plants!

Use this table to record your potato growing adventures and tasting!

Variety	How did you eat it? Mash, chips, roasted, boiled?	Texture score 1–10	Taste score 1–10

BE SAFE!

Do not eat the leaves and stems, they are poisonous. Raw potatoes will also make you very poorly, so always cook them before eating!

TOMATOES

Tomatoes can grow in pots, grow bags, hanging baskets or directly in the ground. You can sow tomatoes in pots on a sunny windowsill, but they can take up lots of space. Buying small plants from your local garden centre is easy and they can go straight outside.

DID YOU KNOW?

You can grow yellow, green and purple tomatoes. Not just red ones!

TIP!

Plant marigold flowers next to your plants. They will help keep away pests, especially aphids and whiteflies. Mint can help keep away pests too.

What to do

1 Fill up your container with compost.

2 Make a hole in the middle of your compost and plant your tomato plant.

3 Water the compost.

4 Tomatoes love sunshine, so place your container in a sunny spot. This can be on a balcony or in your garden.

5 When it's hot outside, water your plants every day and include tomato feed weekly.

6 As your plants grow, you will see flowers form. Tomatoes will grow from these, so look out for the fruits as they start forming.

7 Tomatoes start green, then ripen in the sunshine and change colour. Some tomato varieties like to grow really tall. You can gently tie these plants to a bamboo cane with string, which will help stop them from falling over.

Use this table to record your tomato growing and tasting!

Variety	Sown date	Harvest date	Tasty? Score 1-10!

Find the different tomato varieties hidden in the wordsearch.

- ✳ Tigerella
- ✳ Moneymaker
- ✳ Ferline
- ✳ Beefsteak
- ✳ Marmande
- ✳ Apero
- ✳ Rosella
- ✳ Sunbaby
- ✳ Sungold

N	A	A	K	N	I	S	O	B	N	S	M	T	R
K	N	E	A	A	R	U	E	S	O	O	L	R	L
G	E	R	E	M	O	N	E	E	Y	R	M	N	A
B	T	T	M	E	A	B	E	D	R	I	A	A	N
E	E	A	A	B	L	A	E	N	Y	A	A	U	M
E	U	L	L	L	T	B	S	A	O	A	M	N	S
N	B	L	M	E	O	Y	L	M	O	L	D	F	U
A	M	E	M	A	M	L	Y	R	O	N	M	E	N
P	A	S	N	B	A	L	L	A	L	A	A	R	G
E	Y	O	O	M	T	E	E	M	O	S	L	L	O
R	N	R	A	O	O	M	R	L	M	N	K	I	L
O	R	R	E	K	A	M	Y	E	N	O	M	N	D
B	E	E	F	S	T	E	A	K	S	O	M	E	E
O	T	I	G	E	R	E	L	L	A	G	T	M	O

SWEETCORN

Sweetcorn grows really tall and can be planted outside in your garden.

Did you know that their pollen is carried by the wind instead of bees? Planting sweetcorn in blocks (rather than one long row) helps the wind blow the pollen from one plant to another.

Start sowing your sweetcorn in March or April

1 Fill 7–8 cm pots with multi-purpose compost.

2 Plant one sweetcorn seed per pot, 4 cm deep.

3 Leave on a sunny windowsill. The seeds should germinate within approximately 10 days.

4 In May or June, when your plants are big and strong, take them outside. Plant them in blocks and keep a gap of 60 cm between each plant.

As they grow, keep watering them weekly and flowers called tassels will form at the top of the plants. The tassels make pollen, which blows down onto the threads below and makes the corn cobs grow!

The cobs will grow inside leaves and will be ready when the silks (at the top of the sweetcorn) turn dark brown.

When you think they are ready, gently peel back the leaves and have a look. Have the golden yellow kernels formed yet? If so, twist and pull the cob off at the base!

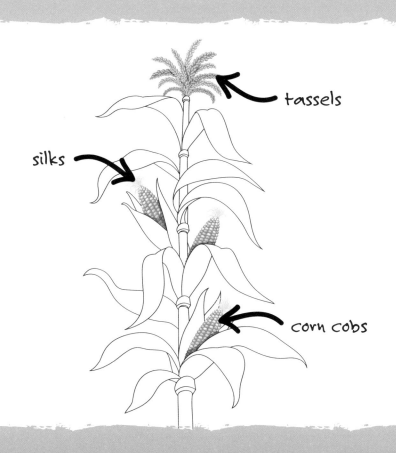

tassels

silks

corn cobs

WILL IT GROW TALLER THAN YOU?

Track the height of you and your sweetcorn.

Ask an adult to measure you and write your name next to your height. As the sweetcorn grows, mark its monthly growth on the chart. When the sweetcorn is fully grown, compare its height to yours!

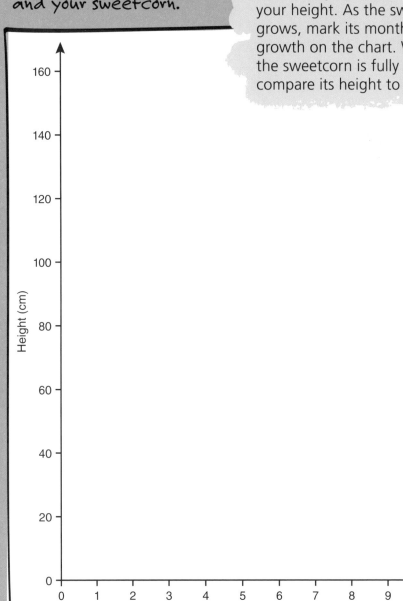

SALAD LEAVES

If you like to see results quickly, then salad leaves are a great vegetable to grow. You can harvest them within 4–6 weeks!

'Rainbow Mixed' chard, 'Red Frills' mustard, 'Lollo Rossa' lettuce, spinach, cress, rocket, chicory and pak choi are all great leaves to grow.

pak choi

red swiss chard

You can pick leaves off the plants when you want to eat them and more will continue to grow.

TIP!

Only take off the outer leaves to eat, as new leaves grow in the middle.

What to do

1 Sprinkle your chosen seeds 1 cm deep in compost, either in a container or directly outside. You can sow these anytime from March to September. Water well!

2 Salad leaves like a sunny but shady spot on a balcony or in a garden, so find a place that has some shade during the day.

3 Keep watering your plants every 2 days and harvest your leaves when they are 10–20 cm tall.

COURGETTES

Courgette plants love lots of water and plenty of sunshine! The plants become big and bushy, forming edible flowers and lots of courgettes.

DID YOU KNOW?

Female courgette flowers need bees and other insects to pollinate them, so that courgettes can form and grow!

You can grow traditional green varieties like 'Defender', stripy ones called 'Eclipse' or round, yellow ones like 'Floridor'.

What to do

1 Courgette seeds need warmth to germinate, so should be started indoors.

2 In May, sow 2 seeds per 8–9 cm pot of compost, pushing the seeds about 2 cm deep. Water well and place them on a sunny windowsill.

3 When your plants are strong and have at least 4–5 leaves, you can plant them outside, either in a large 50 cm container or directly in the ground.

4 Keep your courgette plants 60 cm apart if they are in the ground.

5 Water your courgette plants every 2 days when it's really hot. Give them plenty of water! They also love being fed, so add some tomato feed or your own homemade feed to the watering can every 2 weeks.

TIP!

Harvest your courgettes when they are 15–20 cm long. The quicker you harvest your courgettes, the more will grow.

Record your progress using the table below:

Variety	Sown date	Harvest date	Tasty? Score 1–10!
COURET	March	17\7\2	7

PUMPKINS

Do you love carving pumpkins for Halloween? Read on to find out how to grow your own giant or mini pumpkins perfect for carving.

GET GROWING!

You can grow pumpkin plants in the ground. They form on really long plants called vines.

The vines grow really big and can produce 2–4 pumpkins per plant.

TIP!

Place a tile, piece of wood or sheet of plastic under your growing pumpkins. This will stop them from rotting.

What to do

1 Pumpkin seeds need warmth to germinate, so start them indoors on a sunny windowsill or in a heated greenhouse. You can also buy small plants from your local garden centre if you don't have space inside.

2 In May, sow 2 seeds per 8–9 cm pot of compost, pushing the seeds about 2 cm deep. Water well!

3 When your plants are big and strong with a few leaves, pop them directly in the ground.

4 If you grow more than one plant, keep them at least 1 metre apart.

5 Water around your pumpkin plants every 2 days. If you want your pumpkin to grow really big, add some tomato feed or your own homemade feed to the watering can every 2 weeks.

Pumpkins start off small and green, then gradually change colour to bright orange!

Harvest time!

Your pumpkin is ready to cut off and carve when it is firm and bright orange. It also needs to sound hollow, like a drum. Give it a knock, or tap it with a spoon to see how it sounds.

If your pumpkin looks and sounds ready, you can cut it off using some scissors. Ask an adult for help if you need it.

Use this table to record your adventures growing pumpkins!

Variety	Sown date	Harvest date	Tasty? Score 1–10!

Design your pumpkin carving here.

STRAWBERRIES

Strawberries can be super sweet and juicy, and you can buy many different strawberry plants from your local garden centre. Each plant will give you delicious fruits for 3 years!

Strawberries love a sunny space in your garden or on a balcony. They can be grown directly in the ground or in a container. Perhaps you could grow them in a hanging basket?

What to do

1 Fill up your chosen container with compost.

2 Make a hole big enough for the pot, remove the plant and pop it in its new container or in the ground.

3 Give the compost around your plant lots of water and keep it watered every 3 days.

4 Strawberries love natural plant feed as well, so try making your own on pages 22–23. You can add some to your watering can once a week.

5 Flowers will begin to form on your plant! When they are pollinated by insects, yummy strawberries will begin to grow. They will start tiny and green, then gradually grow bigger and turn red.

6 The bright red colour means that they are ready for picking and eating.

Did you know that you can easily grow lots of new strawberry plants? In the summer, you will see stems called 'runners' coming off your plant and producing a new bud and set of leaves. Keep the runners attached to your plant, but place the bud in its own container and a new plant will form. You could use a pin to hold the runner down in the compost. In 8 weeks, you can cut the runner away from its parent. A free strawberry plant!

RASPBERRIES

Raspberries are like little red jewels that taste delicious!

DID YOU KNOW?

Raspberries grow on woody stems called canes. If planted directly in the ground and looked after well, they can grow to 1 metre tall!

You can buy raspberry canes in your local garden centre during autumn and winter. When you go, you may see 2 types of raspberry canes – summer and autumn varieties.

The variety indicates when they will have yummy fruit for you to pick and eat. They need looking after in different ways as well, so check the label for the right instructions.

What to do

1 Dig one deep hole per raspberry cane. You want it deep enough so all the roots are fully in the ground. Keep your canes about 45 cm apart.

2 Before planting, place a handful of organic matter, either compost or manure, into the hole. This will give your cane a great start.

3 Plant your cane, fill the hole back up with soil and press down gently on the surface of the soil around the cane. This will help your cane stay in position.

4 Give the soil around your canes plenty of water straight away.

5 Water them at least twice a week and add some natural plant feed to their water every 2 weeks.

6 The raspberries are ready to eat when they are bright in colour, feel soft to touch and come off the plant easily. Gently pull one and see if it comes off. If not, leave it a little longer.

Fill in the table below. Don't forget to check the label for how to look after your canes.

Name of raspberry variety	Conditions and help it needs

BLUEBERRIES

Eat blueberries as a yummy snack or add them to a cake or smoothie!

Have you noticed that they have little star shapes on the bottom?

Blueberries grow on round bushes and are great to grow in a large container. They are different to other fruiting plants as they love acidic soil! You can buy the soil in bags at your local garden centre – it will be called ericaceous compost.

What to do

1 Fill up a large container – at least 35 cm wide – with the compost.

2 Make a hole large enough for your potted bush.

3 Remove the bush from the pot and place it in its new container.

4 Give the soil plenty of water and make sure the container is in a sunny spot. Blueberries love the sunshine!

5 Keep watering the soil every 2 days.

As your new bush grows, flowers will form, attracting bees and other insects.

Just like many other fruiting fruits and vegetables, these visitors will pollinate the flowers, making the fruits grow!

You will see your blueberries form, grow and gradually change colour. In late summer, when they are dark blue and looking ready to eat, try to pick one and see if it comes off easily. If so, you can start eating!

In winter, your bushes will lose their leaves, just like raspberries. Don't panic! They are resting before they have to start producing new leaves and fruit the following year. This resting period is called dormancy and it happens with many fruiting plants, trees and bushes.

Use this table to keep track of the different fruits you're growing!

Variety	Sown date	Harvest date	Tasty? Score 1-10!

COMPOSTING

Did you know that you can make your own compost? You don't have to buy it from a garden centre unless you are sowing seeds. Making compost is called composting. Compost is made from fruit and vegetable waste, broken-down old plants, paper and cardboard.

You can buy a compost bin from your local garden centre, or with the help of an adult you can make one using four old wooden pallets.

What can go in your compost bin?

Greens	Browns
Vegetable peelings	Newspaper and paper
Fruit peelings and leftovers	Cardboard
Small weeds and dead plants	Dry autumn leaves
Grass cuttings	Straw

Just pop your peelings, leaves, grass cuttings and small weeds into the top of the bin. Tear the newspaper, cardboard and any large plants into smaller pieces. This will help them break down faster!

Try to make layers of green and brown waste: a layer of brown waste, then some green waste and keep going until you reach the top.

Gradually everything will break down and turn into brown, crumbly compost that should feel moist to touch. Be patient though as it can take up to a year, depending on the size of your bin.

TIP!

Every couple of months you can use a garden fork or trowel to turn everything. If the compost feels soggy, add some more brown material. If it feels really dry, add a little water. Don't worry if you can't reach inside. Perhaps ask an adult to help you check your compost.

Use your homemade compost to fill up your large containers. You can also add a thick layer on top of the soil in the garden. This will feed your plants and slow down any weeds that want to grow!

PESTS

Bees and most butterflies look after your plants, pollinating flowers so that fruits and vegetables grow. Other little creatures are not as helpful and like to damage your plants. You want to try to keep these pests away.

SLUGS AND SNAILS

These slimy critters love eating vegetables, especially leaves! They come out at night and love wet weather so you may miss catching them on your new plants.

If you do see them, pick them up and move them to an open part of your garden. You can try to stop them returning by placing crushed egg shells or sharp sand around your plants. Slugs and snails don't like crawling over a rough surface!

CATERPILLARS

Caterpillars love leaves and flowers! You may see holes in your leaves and petals – this is a sign of caterpillars. They like to hide from you, so look under leaves to try and spot them.

If you do find them, well done! Pick them off and place them away from your plants. Hungry birds will enjoy eating them.

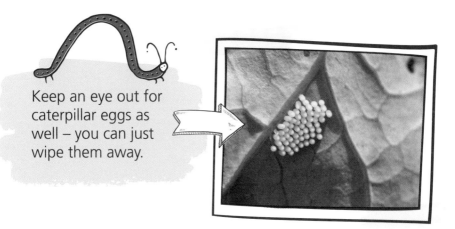

Keep an eye out for caterpillar eggs as well – you can just wipe them away.

FLEA BEETLES

These are tiny creatures, about 2–3 mm in size, that jump around eating holes in leaves. Flea beetles particularly like young brassica and radish leaves.

They love dry conditions, so keep the soil around your plants watered to keep them away. You can also cover your seedlings with netting, which will reduce damage.

APHIDS

Aphids are small insects usually found on the undersides of leaves. The most common are greenfly and blackfly. They weaken your plants by sucking out the liquid inside, called sap. You can use a spray bottle full of water to spray the aphids off the leaves. If some don't fly away, wipe them away using a paper towel or tissue.

COMPANION PLANTING

You can also help keep pests away by planting certain plants together! This is called companion planting.

Plant onions near carrots to discourage carrot fly.

Nasturtiums keep aphids away from beans and cabbage white butterflies away from brassicas.

Marigolds and chives keep aphids away from tomatoes and beans.

marigolds

chives

Mint will help keep away many pests, so keep it in a container nearby.

Become a detective and track your pests' naughty adventures here.

Pest	Date seen	Where?

SAVING SEEDS

Seeds will grow inside some of your vegetables – did you know that you can save these? Each seed is a new free plant for the next year!

BEANS AND PEAS

At the end of the summer when you have nearly picked all of your fresh beans or peas, leave a few pods on the plant. You want them to dry out so they look brown and crispy. When they are ready, you will also be able to hear the seeds rattle inside.

PUMPKINS

The best time to save pumpkin seeds is when you start to carve your spooky creation. You can put your hands inside, have a squelch around, then pull out all the seeds. A spoon will work as well.

Wash the seeds so that they are completely clean, then spread them out on a piece of paper towel. Leave them until they are dry, then place them in a sealed envelope.

You can save seeds from peppers and squashes in the same way.

Do your seeds all look different?
Draw and label the different types here.

TIP!

Write the name of the seeds on the envelope so you don't forget which plant they are from!

HURRAH!

Well done, you have reached the end of the book. You can now definitely grow your own food!

What was your favourite activity?

_____

_____

_____

What was your favourite vegetable to grow? Why?

_____

_____

_____

_____

Who did you grow your fruits and vegetables with?

_____

_____

_____

Draw a picture of you and your homegrown food.

Published by Collins
An imprint of HarperCollins Publishers
Westerhill Road, Bishopbriggs, Glasgow,
G64 2QT

www.harpercollins.co.uk

© HarperCollins Publishers 2020

Collins ® is a registered trademark of
HarperCollins Publishers Ltd.

Text © Annabelle Padwick
Images © Shutterstock.com, except:
p.38: © South Whidbey School Farms
pp.40, 51, 59, 60, 64, 74(t), 78, 82, 86(b),
92(b), 96: © Annabelle Padwick

Publisher: Michelle I'Anson
Project manager: Rachel Allegro
Design: Sarah Duxbury
Typesetter: Jouve
Cover: Kevin Robbins

9780008372699

Printed in China

10 9 8 7 6 5 4 3 2 1

Note from the author:

Writing this book is a dream come true!
If you are reading this, you can achieve
anything if you dream big and stay focused.

Thank you to all the young people I have
met and helped in some way – you have
inspired me so much and guided how I
wrote this book.

Thank you to you for reading this book.
I hope it not only teaches you to grow your
own food, but also builds your confidence
and helps you to believe in yourself.

Lastly, thank you to every parent, auntie,
uncle, grandparent, carer and friend who
chose to pick up and buy this book.

Dream big and have fun.

Annabelle xx